snapshot•picture•library

ELEPHANTS

FOG CITY PRESS

Published by Fog City Press,
a division of Weldon Owen Inc.
415 Jackson Street
San Francisco, CA 94111 USA
www.weldonowen.com

WELDON OWEN INC.

Group Publisher, Bonnier Publishing Group John Owen
President, CEO Terry Newell
Senior VP, International Sales Stuart Laurence
VP, Sales and New Business Development Amy Kaneko
VP, Publisher Roger Shaw
Executive Editor Elizabeth Dougherty
Editorial Assistant Katharine Moore
Associate Creative Director Kelly Booth
Senior Designer William Mack
Designer Michel Gadwa
Production Director Chris Hemesath
Production Manager Michelle Duggan
Color Manager Teri Bell

A WELDON OWEN PRODUCTION
© 2010 Weldon Owen Inc.

Library of Congress Control Number: 2009937745

ISBN 978 1 74089 954 3

10 9 8 7 6 5 4 3 2 1
2010 2011 2012 2013

Printed by Tien Wah Press in Singapore.

Elephants are the biggest animals on land, but they are usually gentle and loving. Female elephants and their young live in large family groups called herds. Often, they stay in these families all their lives.

Most elephants live in the wild in Africa and Asia. Some elephants live in zoos or nature reserves. Wherever they are, elephants eat and drink all the time! They spend their days searching for leaves, twigs, grass, and fruit. Let's follow some elephants around and see what else they like to do!

You can spot an African elephant by its huge, floppy ears. When it's hot, African elephants flap their ears to cool down and flick away pesky insects.

Asian elephants are not as large as their African cousins. They have smaller ears and hairy skin, especially on the tops of their heads.

Elephants that live in the grasslands of Africa walk long distances searching for food and water. They also look for shelter from the hot sun.

Some African
and most Asian
elephants live in
forests, where
there are lots
of plants for
food and trees
for shelter.

To grasp leaves high up in trees, an elephant reaches with its long trunk. It can also stand on its hind legs.

Elephants eat a lot. A single elephant could eat more than a thousand apples in one day!

An elephant uses its trunk to suck
up water. Then it opens its mouth
wide and squirts in the water.

With its trunk,
an elephant
can also smell
things, pick
up food, and
say hello.

Elephants use their trunks to trumpet loudly. Their trunks can pick up the vibrations of another elephant's call from far away.

Elephants' thickly padded feet
can also pick up foot stomps
from other elephants far away.

Elephants cuddle and use their trunks to stroke each other.

Male elephants are called bulls. They live alone or with a few other males. All bulls have tusks.

Tusks are big teeth. They grow longer as an elephant ages. Elephants use their tusks to dig up food and tear bark from trees to eat.

In elephant families, the female relatives live together. The oldest female is the leader. Her daughters, sisters, nieces, and granddaughters all live with her.

When a baby elephant is born, she can weigh as much as a small pony. That's about 220 pounds (100 kg).

Young elephants' mothers and
other older female relatives
feed and care for them.

Most animals stay away from elephants. If a lion comes too close to a baby elephant, the herd will spread their ears and trumpet a warning.

This elephant is tickling his friend with his trunk. Elephants love to play! They roll around in the mud and splash in the water.

When it's hot, it's time for a bath! Elephants take a bath every day to clean their bodies and just to have fun.

For a quick, cool shower, elephants use their trunks as water hoses to suck up water and spray themselves all over.

Mud baths are fun and useful! After the mud dries, it protects the elephant's skin from insects and the heat of the sun.

A dust bath may look messy,
but it also helps protect
an elephant's skin.

Elephants
nap standing
up or leaning
against a tree.
Some elephants
also lie down
to sleep.

Some elephants
are tame. They
can carry things
with their trunks,
and even give
people rides.

Safari parks, zoos, and nature reserves keep elephants safe from hunters. Elephant keepers take good care of the elephants.

In some countries, such as India, people honor elephants. They even dress elephants in colorful costumes on festival days.

In Africa and
Asia, you can
see elephants on
wildlife reserves.
In other countries,
you can visit
elephants in a zoo
or a safari park.
Have you ever
seen an elephant?

African elephants

African elephants are the largest elephants. Both the males and females have tusks. Their backs dip in the middle.

Asian elephants

Asian elephants have domed heads and small ears. There are fewer Asian elephants in the world than African elephants.

Bull elephant

Young male elephants must prepare to leave the herd. As they grow older, males spend more and more time away until they are ready to live alone.

Female elephant

The matriarch is the name for the oldest female elephant in a family. Other adult females help to care for the elephant babies.

Elephant family

A herd of elephants usually contains about six to twelve elephants. When a family gets too large, an older female will begin a new herd.

Baby elephant

Baby elephants drink their mother's milk until they are about four years old. Then they use their trunks to feed themselves.

Feet

Elephants' sensitive feet can pick up vibrations of calls and foot stomps from far away. Stomping herds alert other elephants miles away to trouble.

Tusks

Elephants are right- or left-tusked, just as people are right- or left-handed. They use one tusk more often than the other one, making it shorter.

Trunk

Elephants use their trunks as hands to pick things up. Elephants also use their trunks as snorkels to breathe underwater.

Eating

Elephants eat all the parts of a plant, including the roots and bark. They eat a lot because they only digest about half of what they eat.

Drinking

Every day, elephants drink as much as a bathtub full of water. They suck it up with their trunks and squirt it into their mouths.

Trumpeting

A trumpet is an elephant's loud call when it is excited, angry, or surprised. The elephant raises its trunk in the air and blows through it.

ACKNOWLEDGMENTS

Weldon Owen would like to thank the staff at Toucan Books Ltd, London, for their assistance in the production of this book: Cynthia O'Brien, author and researcher; Ellen Dupont, project editor; and Colin Woodman, designer.